IT'S NOT EASY BEING GREEN

A Black Dartmouth Man's Perspective on
America in Essays, Notes and Letters
2008 – 11

By B.C. Hicks

Cover photo: Michael Poloukhine/The Aegis

"I must be the Blackest Nigga Alive ... they just served me watermelon in jail!!"

- The Author, while awaiting a court appearance in CT

"He was born poor, died rich and didn't hurt anyone along the way."

- Duke Ellington on Louis Armstrong

Contents

1- INTRODUCTION

People from my era at Dartmouth College will recall a day-long "Rap on Race" that was held between students, faculty and administration after shanties that had been erected on the Green to protest the College's support of South Africa's apartheid regime were sledgehammered by students calling themselves conservatives. The attack on the shanties occurred at night while protesters were sleeping inside of them – a clear violation of Dartmouth's sacred "principle of community."

Unfortunately, for Dartmouth people and Americans in general, discussions such as the "Rap on Race" are precipitated by emergencies and take place infrequently. After the crisis has passed, comments raised fade into memory and life proceeds as it always has.

For black Ivy Leaguers, black corporate Americans and blacks at the highest levels of government, race is always top-of-mind because, too often, the white people they encounter in these environments presume themselves to be superior, better qualified and more entitled to raises & promotions. Tradition and the old-boy network support this way of thinking.

The essay collection I wrote entitled, <u>SUPERIORITY COMPLEX</u>: <u>My Life as a Black Fair-Haired Boy at Time Inc.</u>, provides many examples of a media company, tasked with increasing knowledge and encouraging input from all sources, instead acting to keep mediocre white males in the elite and terminating black employees who dare to raise "inconvenient truths" about Time Inc.'s culture and the unhealthy, uninformed racial attitudes that prevail in that company, elsewhere in the media and entertainment industry, and throughout corporate America.

Those essays were filed with the Library of Congress in 1995, more than a decade in advance of Barack Obama's historic run for the White House, but the issues and problems raised in my writing are as real and persistent today as they were almost 17 years ago. A case in point: Michelle Obama's Princeton thesis describing the two social worlds (one black, one white) that she inhabited as a black Ivy Leaguer in the 1980s made so much news during the 2008 Presidential campaign that Princeton made it unsearchable in their database. The university's action supports Attorney General Eric Holder's remark that Americans are "cowards" when it comes to addressing the issue of race.

Ralph Ellison's 1952 novel <u>Invisible Man</u> inspires the work I do as a multi-media crusader for racial understanding in American society and the American workplace. I represent a black business constituency, the military and the Ivy League, and I believe this essay collection will spark continuing discussion and debate as to whether or not we live in a "post-racial society" now that a black man and his family occupy the White House.

Because the Obamas continue to face charges of "elitism" for speaking like educated people and because Herman Cain must contend with a "high-tech lynching" effort aimed at his candidacy for the Republican nomination, I believe that Americans have a long way to go before we can make the claim that "race is no longer an issue" in this country.

Through magazine & newspaper op-eds, by addressing business groups and by creating programs for radio, television & film, Invisible Man Enterprises is helping this country reconcile its paradoxical love of democracy on the one hand and its reverence for hierarchies (usually headed by white males) on the other.

America is as close as history has come to a society that rewards its citizens based solely on the contributions they make to the nation's economy. Invisible Man Enterprises is committed to ensuring that merit and excellence prevail over tradition and cronyism in this promising, but still very young experiment in democracy we know as the United States of America.

New York, NY

November, 2011

2- THE BURDEN

During the fall of my senior year at Ridgewood (NJ) High School, John Clark, Dartmouth Class of '62, drove me and two other Ridgewood students up to New Hampshire for an informal look at Dartmouth College. One Friday afternoon, we were unceremoniously dropped at the dormitories of freshmen from Northern New Jersey with instructions to meet Mr. Clark and his wife at Thayer Dining Hall at noon on Sunday.

Dennis McCooe, Class of '86, was my host for what turned out to be Homecoming Weekend, featuring the Dartmouth vs. Harvard football game and the infamous fraternity parties I had been warned to stay away from. The day we arrived, the freshmen were building a structure out of railroad ties that would be set ablaze during a Dartmouth Night celebration in front of adoring students, alumni and more than a few prospectives and "randoms" trying to pass themselves off as students.

Some knucklehead I knew in high school had convinced me that beer is an acquired taste, so I decided to use my time away from parental supervision wisely. I found a keg in my host's dorm, New Hampshire Hall, and tried to acquire a taste for beer in one sitting. When Sunday finally rolled around, I had drunk more than my share of Homecoming Weekend beers and still didn't like the taste. I felt like a moderate drinker who overindulges on New Year's Eve and wakes up with an ice pack on his head in a place he doesn't remember traveling to. The last thing I wanted to do was get into a car with two hungover classmates and two perfectly lucid adults and drive 4-1/2 hours back to New Jersey. Still, I decided that once I got back home, I would immediately get to work on my Dartmouth College application.

As a high school senior, I was torn between pursuing the wide-open possibilities of civilian life and the discipline of military life. The U.S. Naval Academy at Annapolis was as beautiful a campus as I had seen anywhere, but after my weekend at Dartmouth, I viewed life differently. I decided that I had followed orders from my parents all my life and a career in the military seemed to offer more of the same. Dartmouth looked like a place where I would be free to have fun and get a top-notch education at the same time. Writing out my application,

I was nagged by the question: "Who comes first, myself or my country?", but Homecoming Weekend convinced me that if it came down to a choice between Dartmouth and Annapolis, I would choose Dartmouth.

My Dartmouth application was as clear a portrait of myself as was possible at that time. I was very proud of myself for the job I did on the application – and even more proud (and a little scared) when the acceptance letter arrived.

By the time I arrived at Dartmouth College, I was burnt out academically. I felt I had combated the "blacks are intellectually inferior" stereotype my entire life and had nothing but enemies to show for it.

Four years was as long as I had ever stayed in one place, so I wanted to make the most of the four years I was about to spend at Dartmouth. What I wanted out of my Dartmouth experience was a group of friends that I would know and respect forever. I also wanted to read great books by great authors and, through them, gain greater insight into my own life. My four- year plan was to study whatever interested me, come away with a close-knit group of friends and get hired by a company that would pay me to acquire the skills I would need to succeed in business.

When I walked onto campus with a social agenda that superseded my academic agenda, I embarked on an approach to college and to life that required a high tolerance for risk. During my era, there were nearly 30 different fraternities, sororities and co-ed fraternal organizations at Dartmouth. My contemporaries and I spent a lot of time in fraternity basements sizing up egos and knocking back beers over games of pong. Nearly every fraternity had a modified ping pong table in its basement – always within easy reach of the taps. Each fraternity had developed its unique approach to pong, a drinking game that tests the reflexes, wit and capacity of the players. I have college friends who will look back nostalgically and say that they learned as much about people and life over beers on the pong table as they learned in classrooms.

I'm sure that this approach to college life was as addictive as some narcotics – although things could get pretty stressful during mid-terms and finals. In order to continue in this lifestyle and keep up with my peers, I had to pass my classes and justify my parents' expenditures every term. I could cite many examples of Dartmouth classmates who had failed or cheated or for some other reason ended up expelled or on a five-year plan. I was determined not to become a statistic. I often absorbed the entire syllabus for all of my classes over a three- or four-day period – and then got tested on the material shortly afterwards. Fortunately, the courses I took were more likely to feature essay questions as opposed to questions with answers that were absolutely right or absolutely wrong. It was often possible to choose from among several essay topics and thereby demonstrate that I had read at least some of the things that the professor decided to put on the test. The trick during reading period was to decide which things to read from each syllabus and how much time to devote to each class. Of course, there was never enough time to read every item on every reading list, so I inevitably walked into a mid-term or a final with at least one flank undefended. The chilling sensation one feels when confronted with a test question that reveals a weakness in one's test preparation is nearly indescribable. It's a combination of terror and panic that has been known to produce tears in some instances. However, I've been amazed at what the human mind has been able to accomplish at the precise moment that financial pressure, peer pressure and test pressure have brought me to the brink of a mental meltdown. With an empty blue book on my desk and the clock ticking, some essay tests have forced me to a level of lyricism that would challenge the skills of even the best freestyle rappers.

As committed as I was to getting what I wanted out of Dartmouth in the way I wanted to get it, my approach was far from guilt-free. From grade school though high school, A's had been the norm, not the exception for me, but that trend came to an abrupt halt starting with my first term in college. I knew I wasn't putting in the effort that I was capable of on the academic front, and this baffled and frustrated my mother. When my parents' divorce seemed imminent, my mother left her first love, teaching, to become a stock broker so there would be enough money to put me through the kind of college she knew I could get into. The combined stresses of single parenthood, her job and my sophomoric rebelliousness proved too much for her. My mother died suddenly and unexpectedly, of a brain aneurysm, on December 30, 1984. She was 45 years old.

I was a 19-year-old Dartmouth College sophomore. I was keenly determined to graduate on time and equally determined to continue learning about human nature over games of beer pong. To everyone except those closest to me, it seemed that I was headed straight to the top. I was an intelligent and assimilated young black man on his way to becoming the first person in his family with an Ivy League education. To me and those closest to me, I looked like damaged goods. I had been an over-achiever all of my life, but now, with my family's money betting on me to win – all I could manage was a pretty pathetic show. My family thought I was trying so hard to impress my white friends that I ended up neglecting my responsibilities to myself. I was an academic also-ran in an environment where the conservative Dartmouth *Review* survived and flourished. The *Review* is a newspaper that is famous for asserting in ways subtle and not-so-subtle that blacks are intellectually inferior. I couldn't be sure which of the white friends I clung to so faithfully subscribed to the *Review's* proselytizing, but I had decided to fight my war in fraternity basements instead of classrooms – and nothing was going to force me to change my tactics.

I was in a prison of my own making, and I wasn't sure if I had what it took to get out.

3- LETTER TO *THE NEW YORKER*

February 17, 2009

Mr. David Remnick, Editor

The New Yorker

4 Times Square

New York, NY 10036

Mr. Remnick:

I have started a management & diversity consulting business that will produce tangible results and thereby beat those opportunists @ Diversity Inc. at their own game.

Part of my practice will involve writing articles for magazines that are read by more than just HR and "Diversity" officers, and I would like to speak with you about excerpting my book or commissioning new pieces from me that would run in *The New Yorker*.

Nobody that I know of in the media is as qualified as I am to address the issue of race relations within companies because no casualty of a failed or abandoned diversity effort has persevered in the fight for as long as I have. Most give up whatever hopes they had of becoming CEO or being their own boss & just settle for being an employee somewhere.

Now that the Barack Obama era has begun, it is high time for my writing to appear – and *The New Yorker* is the right magazine to publish me.

Please read through the enclosed materials and expect my call.

Best,

B. C. Hicks

4- Letter to Princeton University

Mary Ann,

3/8/09

As far back as January, 1990, my former boss, FORTUNE Publisher James B. Hayes, asked me where I thought the next great black civil rights leader would come from.

My answer, as you will see in one of the attachments, was that the business world would produce that person. Corporate America is where Jim Crow is making his last stand, and it takes people like me, with experience in both corporate America and a chocolate city (Newark, NJ) to defy stereotypes and increase racial understanding between communities that are growing increasingly segregated in this society. For anecdotal evidence of this point, seek out the article, "Will You Be My Black Friend?," by Devin Friedman, GQ (November, 2008)

My new company, Invisible Man Enterprises, will pursue the fight on four basic fronts:

1) as a management consultant, helping corporations devise and implement diversity initiatives.

2) as the author of magazine articles, newspaper op-eds, and my Time Inc. employment memoir.

3) as a business school professor (and this is an area where Dr. [Cornel] West might be helpful); I have devised a course, "Fostering Communication Between the Races in Society and in the Workplace," that I would like to teach as a faculty member at both NYU-Stern and Columbia Business School.

4) as a producer of educational and entertainment projects for the stage and screen exploring issues of race relations in America. (Just this week, I met Alex Gibney, director of the Oscar-winning documentary "Taxi to the Dark Side," about prisoner abuse in Bagram and Abu Ghraib prisons – and pitched him the idea of delving into the history of diversity initiatives at my former employer, Time Warner).

I am reading "Democracy Matters," I read "Race Matters" when it came out, and I heard Dr. West speak at Time Warner's old headquarters building, 75 Rockefeller, when I was working at Vibe during that magazine's first year.

I would like to schedule a trip to Princeton to meet with

Dr. West and was hoping you could facilitate that. (Also, I was hoping you could persuade Dr. West to share these materials with his literary agent.)

Thank you.

Best,

B. C. Hicks

Invisible Man Enterprises

5- LETTER TO VANITY FAIR

March 10, 2009

Ms. Bethany McLean

Vanity Fair

4 Times Square

New York, NY 10036

Dear Bethany:

Last week, I met Alex Gibney, your collaborator on "ENRON: The Smartest Guys in the Room," and pitched him the idea of looking into diversity efforts at Time Warner and the other big media companies.

To add to my story: I was Tiger Woods at Time Inc. long before the real Tiger came along & damaged the notion of white supremacy in this country with his runaway victory at the 1997 Masters.

In spite of the excellent work I produced at FORTUNE and Vibe, the culture at Time Inc. refused to acknowledge that a Dartmouth-educated black person, when given the chance, could outperform his preppy white peers.

Time Inc. didn't exactly fire me, but they did make it

impossible for me to stay at FORTUNE … then at Vibe, they told me that in order to stay with the company, I had to relocate to Detroit & assume responsibility for that magazine's sales efforts to the Big Three automakers.

When I wrote my book & tried to get it published years ago, Time Inc. refused to acknowledge or address the shortcomings I pointed out and instead countered the charges I made with the claim that I am grandiose, delusional, suffering from bi-polar disorder and in need of hospitalization. Really what I needed was a job and the freedom to pursue my career without being harassed by lazy & incompetent white people trying to protect their spots in the pecking order.

Today, my former Time Inc. co-workers at DiversityInc. are abusing the legal system with a frivolous lawsuit against me. (Brief enclosed).

If you think this adds to the case for a documentary about diversity at Time Inc./Time Warner, please share it with Alex Gibney.

Any assistance you can provide in this area would be greatly appreciated.

Best,

B. C. Hicks

6- Demystifying & Destygmatizing Depression

I.

The problems of this world are so large and so pervasive that I think there's something wrong with you if you *don't* end up in Bellevue or on a psychiatrist's couch from time to time. One of those tough-guy footballisms that stuck with me through the years is that "aggressive mistakes aren't mistakes." I suggest that if you don't seek help one day – be it at a hospital or a 12- step program, whether you arrive voluntarily or in restraints – it means that you are not going about your life aggressively enough, and you're not making enough mistakes.

In hospitals, often the first question I was asked by the psychiatrist would be: "What does the expression, 'People who live in glass houses shouldn't throw stones' mean to you?"

My answer was and is essentially The Golden Rule:

"Do unto others as you would have them do unto you." Here, I would carry it one step further and say that the media, communications and technology explosion has created a world in which we all essentially *do* live in glass houses.

An early piece of advice I received from Jim Hayes was to do nothing in my business or personal life that I would be ashamed to read about on the front page of the New York *Times*.

Alright, so I spent some time in Bellevue. So did a fellow claiming to be Santa Claus in a movie called "Miracle on 34th Street." If he can live with the stigma, so can I.

During my weeks as a patient in locked psychiatric units, I noticed that patients develop a connection with each other that they crave, but almost never achieve, with their doctors. On the unit, we spent much of our time in conversation with other patients – often rehearsing what we planned to say to our psychiatrists when we got the chance. These conversations enabled us to temporarily step outside of our own preoccupations and listen very carefully to the concerns of another patient. Many of my compatriots agree that the mutual respect that develops between two people making an honest effort to communicate existed between patients, but was absent from the patient/doctor exchange. Part of the problem is that doctors assume that because they went to medical school, they have all the answers. Too often in sessions, patients do all of the talking while psychiatrists sit silently in judgment. "Am I showing any signs of improvement, doctor?" Silence. The only way to get any kind of reaction from these characters is to tell them that you think you can cope without medication. It was exceedingly frustrating when communications would break down at this point and the pronouncement from on high would be: "difficult" or "manic" or "depressed" or "mentally ill."

Normal people place entirely too much stock in doctors' fancy MD or Ph.D. degrees, which complicates things further.

I'd like to see how those psychiatrists would deal with the stress of being the head of a household and receiving the news that the comfortable status that they had studied and worked so hard to achieve would suddenly be stripped away from them. Hospitals, insurance companies and rich, neurotic patients could no longer be relied upon for money because, for a good reason or for no good reason at all, the medical profession is now off-limits to them. Sure, these former psychiatrists would still *own* their expensively-framed sheepskins that they aspired toward for as long as they could remember, and sure, they would still be people of good character who neither anticipated nor deserved such a ruinous change in fortunes – but no amount of consoling would change the compelling fact that now they're nothing more or less than unskilled, unemployed people living well beyond their means. Now these fine people would be confronted with a dilemma. Choice number one: hold fast to the high standards they've set for themselves for their entire lives and do whatever it takes – legal or illegal – to maintain themselves and their families in the comfortable lifestyle that a psychiatrist's income had made possible. (This route might lead its followers to be characterized as having a tendency toward "mania.") Choice number two: scale hopes and expectations back somewhat, live like a miser – or worse, a beggar or a ho – and perhaps sell off some assets to put money in your pocket, food on the table, shoes on your feet, clothes on your back and a roof over your head. Such a withdrawal from cherished luxuries usually involves withdrawal from cherished friends due to the embarrassing contrast between what is and what was. (This second route might lead Ph.Ds and MDs to diagnose in its followers a tendency toward "depression.") A third group of people might have good and bad days, thinking sometimes that they'll become wildly rich in spite of the fact that medicine is no longer an option for them; at other times they're down in the dumps and unable to get out of bed because they've never known life without medicine or life with failure and so would rather face the certainty of suicide than a future they can't imagine. (These vacillators are said to suffer from "manic depression.")

A sudden change in circumstances that invalidates all the accomplishments you've achieved in the past and threatens to ruin you in the not-too-distant future can cause your mind to play some cruel tricks on you. If you're concerned about losing your apartment, for example, you might dream or imagine that a wrecking ball had demolished the entire building that you live in. Now, under normal circumstances, the same idea might occur to you while you're at work. Eventually, reality would intrude, your terrible vision would fade into memory as quickly as it arrived and, for the rest of the day, you'd be up to your ears in the business at hand.

When you're unemployed and a high achiever, your dreams and visions compete on equal footing with reality. If something beyond your control had suddenly and wrongly taken you away from your life's work, it wouldn't be so difficult to believe that something beyond your control had suddenly and indiscriminately wiped out something you'd worked all your life to acquire. Now here's the tricky part: when you're delusional, the difference between imagining an event and actually *witnessing* or *experiencing* that event no longer exists. That's why we writers send a lot of letters and faxes. It's pleasant to think that our persuasiveness comes across in print and actually causes things to happen – even though, unbeknownst to us – the addressee is on an extended vacation and our beautifully crafted letter remains sitting, unopened and harmless, in the mailbox. The feeling that people are dropping what they're doing to act on what you *want* them to act upon as a direct result of something you've written or said is deliciously euphoric – but it's also sometimes dangerous. Which leads me back to my point at the top about the importance of being able to recognize that you might be making some aggressive mistakes. You need help if there's a variance between what's really happening in this world and what you *perceive* to be happening in this world. The kind of help I'm advocating is the "talking cure," which was once in vogue – because I don't think you're necessarily ill if you're delusional. Mania, depression and manic depression are healthy responses to the hypothetical disaster I described above. In my opinion, you are sick if you continue along on an even keel when conditions in your life quickly change from normal to radically abnormal.

But that's just me. The doctors, psychologists and psychopharmacologists who run the system think differently, and I think that's a problem. They haven't yet appreciated the wisdom in the saying, "The inmates are running the asylum." Rather than medicate away perfectly normal human responses to unnatural occurrences in life, why not spend time during therapy endeavoring to isolate those stressors in life that landed the patient in the hospital or outpatient group in the first place? Working with skilled facilitators and other patients who find themselves in analogous situations, patients might see that they themselves can conceive of a work and/or living situation that will be absent the unhealthy influences that currently plague them. Let's refer back to our hypothetical for a second. If our recently dispossessed psychiatrists feel that they have been unjustly separated from their livelihoods, it would be neither unusual nor unnatural for the manics in the bunch to "take arms against a sea of troubles" and look for ways to convince the powers that be to allow them to pursue their life's work. If they feel that *racism* played a role in their ouster, they'll never prevail in their effort using rational tactics alone for the simple reason that racism itself ain't rational. This accounts for my circulating the rumor that I had been named Chairman of Time Inc.

During a conversation in which I told a woman I had interviewed with in Conde Nast Human Resources that I would succeed Reg Brack as Chairman, she asked, "Are you delusional?" I paused and thought to myself, "That's a good question." When, during my quest for the job of Chairman, Vibe Publisher or virtually any other role at Time Inc. that would sufficiently challenge my faculties I couldn't distinguish reality from my own crazy-like-a-fox bullshit tactics – exhausted and confused – I checked myself into the emergency room of St. Vincent's Hospital in the West Village and, on another occasion, Norwalk

Hospital in Norwalk, CT. On these occasions, my mind was doing things to me that I had never seen happen before and I needed relief. With the benefit of hindsight, I now know that my delusions had crossed the line into the realm of psychosis – which is a whole *other* kind of trip. I had been writing letters – angry letters – to the top people in the company, incorporating quotes from Malcolm X, quotes from jazz critics and quotes from any other source that I felt might convince them that I deserved a shot at continuing my career at Time Warner. I was bullish on the company. When things had been going well for me at FORTUNE, I elected to put 100% of my 401(k) money into Time Warner stock – and it was my ambition then to rise to a level in the company where my efforts would have an impact on the company's stock price. With the kind of sales results I was generating at FORTUNE and the access I had as a FORTUNE sales rep to top business people in America and around the world, I knew that when the time was right I'd be able to pursue my goal of trading in my office in the Time & Life Building for a larger one at 75 Rockefeller. I had no respect for Reg Brack – not only because of his backward stance on the diversity issue, but also because I felt that any Chairman of Time Inc. who couldn't finagle a seat for himself on the Time Warner board was nothing more than an empty suit. During my job hunt, I was trying to land virtually anything that would enable me to satisfy the immediate need to pay my bills. I had shelved the longer-term goal of a big-time job at Time Warner for the time being: I was too busy trying to prove that there really is "Life After Death," as Biggie Smalls put it.

II.

A good friend of mine once told me that hospitals are places to go in order to get better. That axiom seems to hold true for every ailment except psychiatric disorders. The medical establishment must believe that mania, depression and manic depression are incurable because all of the psychiatrists I've encountered are in love with the idea of keeping me medicated for the rest of my life. Now, what do you think *that* does to the perception of psychiatric illness among normal people? Ironically, I think it's the hideous side effects that accompanied earlier psychiatric medications that has created such a lasting, negative image of people suffering from psychiatric disorders. I know that medications have improved over the years, but that doesn't mean I want to be on them forever – especially if the stress from my life is gone and I no longer exhibit the kind of behavior I did when I was under pressure. Someone besides me must be benefitting from keeping me on medications in perpetuity – and I suspect the psychiatrists and pharmaceutical companies get more out of the arrangement than I. So now I say, thanks doc for all of your help when I needed you – but it's time for you to look elsewhere for your laboratory animals. I'm finished testing medicines for the advancement of science.

Notes written to myself while a patient at Eye-6, a locked psychiatric unit at Columbia Presbyterian Medical Center

- The underlying assumption in psychiatric wards: patients are admitted because they are undergoing a *crisis* of some sort in their lives.
- Root meaning of the word crisis: *change*
- The hospital's assumption is that this change is always a change for the worse ... therein lies the root of the problem ... topics like "Non-compliance with medications" are discussed, rather than "Are medications necessary in the first place?"

- *The challenge:* To prove that the symptoms I exhibited were caused by external factors (racism in the workplace) rather than internal factors (bipolar disorder/manic depression)

After I recounted some of my adventures as a psych patient, a friend of mine told me that she wished her schedule would permit her to go to group therapy. I told her that she really should try to make the time – even if she ignored the therapeutic aspects and focused solely on the networking opportunities.

America is often referred to as the great melting pot, and I would argue that some of the best melting pots in American society are jails, psychiatric units and outpatient therapy groups. People from all strata of society are stripped of their identification, their clothing and other trappings from the outside world and are forced to deal with each other as equals.

On psych units, patients spend their days in supervised group activities like arts and crafts, personal grooming, AA meetings, current events discussions, calisthenics and the like. When it's not mealtime (the highlight of the day), and when we aren't engaged in informal conversation with other patients, there's plenty of time to spend alone and reflect upon events from our past that may have contributed to whatever was bothering us at the moment or anything that had ever bothered us at any point in our lives. For the sake of our own sanity, we would keep these thoughts to ourselves – vowing never to share them with our psychiatrists, lest they betray our trust and prescribe more medication.

As crazy as it sounds, I used some of this time to analyze my feelings about (former FORTUNE Advertising Sales Director) Stu Arnold's suggestion that I "learn to forgive my father."

Because of my parents' divorce, I rarely saw my father when I was in my late teens, and he really didn't play much of a role in my life until I entered my early 30s and was faced with an employment situation and a divorce that had thrown my life into turmoil.

My father's second marriage was to a white woman with a history of psychiatric problems. She committed suicide soon after they were married. For many years, I considered my father a failure as a family man, and during my most private moments in the hospital, I was able to pinpoint the source of my anger.

Once, during a conversation in which my father tried

to parent me by phone from his home outside of Washington, DC, I cut him short by telling him that I considered us to be peers. He had chosen to pursue a career in the military; I had chosen a career at Time Inc. Both were valid paths, but neither was superior, to my way of looking at things.

...

Rhoda R., the mother of my son David and my estranged wife at the time of this writing, refused to allow first Bellevue Hospital and later Columbia-Presbyterian Medical Center to release me into her care. This forced me to convalesce at the home of my maternal grandmother, Ms. Pauline, in a rough section of Newark, NJ.

My grandmother is a GM retiree and a lifelong resident of Newark. Although she never went to high school, my grandmother was a successful Newark bar owner for over 20 years. The first, Pauline's Corner, was located at 16th Avenue and South 18th Street. The second, Devil's Hideaway, was at 19th Avenue and South 19th Street.

A familiar refrain of my grandmother's: "There ain't no fence around the ghetto keeping folks in. If people want to leave, they should just get up and go." Bars, cocktail parties, jails and psych units are venues where lots of good conversations take place. All parties to those conversations can come away smarter if they take the time to listen. That goes for you, too, doctors.

You didn't learn everything there is to know about life as a 20- something medical student, and you don't know everything now. I'd rather listen to my grandmother than listen to you.

Every Sunday morning at 7 o'clock, my grandmother gets the Sunday *Star-Ledger* and checks the ads for specials at Shop Rite, FoodTown and other area supermarkets. After the "easy come, easy go" spending philosophy I had practiced as a yuppie in New York, foodshopping with my grandmother was a truly excruciating experience. She never purchased name brands and never purchased items in one store that were cheaper that week in another store across town. My grandmother even got "rain checks" for discounted items that had sold out.

My grandmother gets her news from the free TV stations, and weekdays are not complete without *Judge Judy* at 4pm, the second half of *The People's Court* (Judge

Ed Koch presiding) at 4:30, *Jeopardy!* at 7pm and *The Fresh Prince of Bel Air* at 7:30.

In November and December, 1997, my grandmother took time away from her job at the Newark Museum to look after me and to satisfy herself that I had acquired enough domestic skills to raise David on my own.

Another familiar refrain: "I ain't got nothin', but what I have I'd like to give to you now when I'm around to see it." There's a sincerity and a depth to her love for me that I am unable to describe or to quantify. All I can say is that it's the most powerful healing force that I know.

7- Can We Talk?

4/20/09

It's not your fault that you don't see the world the way I do … it's because you can't.

I'm realizing now that precious few, if any, can … because nobody has lived my life … and no one has pushed himself or herself to the limits I have.

"Live Free or Die" is the New Hampshire state motto.

Once, when I was a patient on a locked psych unit in Westport, CT, I couldn't for the life of me understand why I was being held there -- and I couldn't make the doctors, nurses or hospital administrators understand how urgently I needed to get out.

When nothing seemed to be going my way, I became convinced that I was going to die in captivity – of old age.

For someone who grew up singing the refrain:

"Give me land, lots of land Under starry skies above … Don't fence me in …", the prospect of dying on a psych ward – and waiting years for my death to come (because I was fairly young and in reasonably good shape) – was something I was determined not to do.

So, on more than one occasion, as a patient at Hall-Brooke in Westport, CT, I started a fight with security personnel and got wrestled to the ground, fully expecting to receive a lethal injection when I was immobilized on the floor.

I am a professional communicator, and I wasn't getting through. I knew, however, that somewhere in this world there existed a complete version of a manuscript I had written, chronicling my adventures as a "black fair-haired boy at Time Inc.," and, when it was discovered, perhaps years after my death, I knew the racist fucking psychiatric community would get the thumb in its eye that it so richly deserves.

Perhaps now there can be some honest and constructive steps taken toward dismantling psychiatry altogether ... or, at the very least, putting those smug MDs below psychologists, nurses, social workers and therapists (did I leave anybody out?) in the chain of command.

8- AN OPEN LETTER TO MY FATHER

4/19/09

Back to the hospital, you say?

For what purpose?

I've been there, motherfucker. What about you?

The first person to recommend hospitalization or medication for me is the last person who will take that advice for himself.

Besides, a white doctor can't get inside a black man's head. I think after 14 years, that's been established. A white doctor sees me as inferior just like my own father does. So fuck him and fuck you.

You say you read a lot of books and that makes you smart? Try meeting the authors of the books you read and matching wits with them in real time. That's what true intellectuals do … it's what two of my heroes, Ernest Hemingway and Miles Davis, did on separate occasions as expatriates in Paris … and it's what I've been doing for as long as I can remember.

And I'm curious about what it is that prevents you from seeing me as Barack Obama's peer. Is it because he's been published and he's famous? Is that your measure of success after all the reading you've done? The *American Idol* definition of achievement?

Take that trite piece of garbage *The Audacity of Hope* or, by most accounts, his superior freshman effort, *Dreams of My Father,* and put it next to anything I've written within the past few weeks or months.

No magazine, book or newspaper editor in the country will tell you that Barack Obama is a better writer than I am ... so why do you persist with the inferiority complex? If you still think the fruit of your loins can't succeed on his own terms in this society, Mr. Arthur Conan Doyle fan, then you are failing to see the evidence that is so apparent to everyone else. And if that's the case, "I can't do nothin' for you, man," as Flava Flav put it so beautifully on the cd *Fear of a Black Planet* by Public Enemy.

Well, don't let me keep you. Stick your nose back into your book, if that's what makes you feel smart and proud of yourself. Meanwhile, the real world is passing you by – dinosaur.

9- LETTER TO FORMER DARTMOUTH PRESIDENT JIM WRIGHT

February 23, 2009

Mr. James Wright

President

Dartmouth College

Hanover, NH 03755

President Wright:

I have recently started a management & diversity consulting business, Invisible Man Enterprises, and I need your help in making it and myself into a multi-media crusader for racial understanding in American society and the American workplace.

In my role as a consultant, I will help companies devise and implement diversity initiatives.

Drawing on my skills earned as an English BA at Dartmouth, I will author magazine and newspaper articles on the subject.

Finally, and this is where you come in, I plan to become a business school professor and stress the importance of workplace diversity to a wide variety of audiences. I have already submitted an application to NYU's School of Continuing and Professional Studies, but any assistance you can provide in opening doors at NYU's Stern School of Business and Columbia Business School would be greatly appreciated.

I am an Air Force brat who grew up black in officer housing on military bases across the country. For as long as I can remember, I have been creating diversity just by walking into a room. Also, my family relocated often when I was growing up, so I was constantly forced to adapt to new academic and social environments.

All of this change was difficult for me at the time it was happening, but it proved to be great training for my career as an advertising salesperson at Time Inc. I worked at FORTUNE magazine and at Vibe (Quincy Jones' urban music publication) and proved unable to rise in the company due to my colleagues' uneasiness around a black person who was more comfortable around whites than they were around blacks.

I wrote a book of essays on the subject that has been

complete and ready for publication for over 10 years. Now that Invisible Man Enterprises is up and running and the Barack Obama era has begun, I believe the climate is right for my book to be released. As I have said in query letters to literary agents and publishers, corporate America is where Jim Crow is making his last stand. As a management consultant, writer and professor, it will be my job to bring a unique perspective to this issue and to bring sunshine to the all-too-often ignored fact that those who write and edit the large-circulation magazines and newspapers in this country tend to be white and out of touch with a browning population. For evidence, seek out and read the recent GQ article, "Will You Be My Black Friend?", by Devin Friedman. (It's in the issue with Jimmy Kimmel on the cover).

For the entire 10+ years my book has been written, it has been sitting in the files at the Dartmouth Alumni Magazine. A profile of myself, my business and my writing in that publication is long overdue. Please use your influence with the writers and editors of the Dartmouth Alumni Magazine to have them contact me with the purpose of writing an article at least as long as the one devoted to my former roommate and Dartmouth legacy Kurt Schneider, '87, who is now CEO of the Harlem Globetrotters.

Thanks in advance for your attention to these concerns. I will be in contact with you soon.

Best regards,

B. C. Hicks

10- EMAIL EXCHANGE

--- On Thu, 3/12/09, Hermann Mazard wrote:

From: Hermann Mazard

Subject: Re: Important Enclosure from Dartmouth College

To: "B. C. Hicks"

Cc: Lauren.H.Cummings@Dartmouth.EDU, "Nelson Armstrong" Date: Thursday, March 12, 2009, 4:31 PM

B. C.,

While I support the spirit of your message, I cannot condone the manner in which you are going about raising awareness for the issue. Please cease and desist any and all hostile behavior.

You did not get a Letter of Trespass from the College because of the contents of your messages; you most likely received it because you packaged it in a menacing and threatening manner.

I am your classmate and friend. Please heed this warning to cease and desist all hostile activity. The more you escalate the manner in which you communicate, the less attention your concerns stand to ever get.

Warmly yours, Hermann

D'87

Hermann,

All I did was express my displeasure at hearing back from an assistant instead of the president, who I addressed my letter to. Wright is a mental midget, and never should have been President of Dartmouth College.

He taught "Cowboys & Indians," the easiest A in the catalog.

He showed zero intellectual curiosity by appointing Holly Sateia, a white woman, to head diversity efforts at the College ... and appointing zero blacks to his direct-reports list.

B. C. Hicks

11- DREAM BIG

How's this for an observation

4/20/09

When you're young, you're taught to dream big -- that if you apply yourself in school, the only limits on your life will be the boundaries of your imagination.

Think Dr. Seuss, **"Oh, The Places You'll Go."**

As we age, however, outsized ambition becomes unseemly. Gradually, it's more important for us to appear humble, polite & respectful of authority figures and chains of command.

Well, that message never sunk in for me.

Whenever I run into a snag at any point in my life, I appeal to the wisdom in George Benson's tune **"The Greatest Love of All."**

My favorite passage is: **"I believe the children are our future...**

Teach them well and let them lead the way ... Show them all the beauty they possess inside ... And give them a sense of pride..."

Later, and more relevant to the way this message started, the song says:

"Everybody's searching for a hero ... People need someone to look up to.

I never found anyone who fulfilled my needs. A lonely place to be.

So I learned to depend on me."

12- RUMOR STARTED

Where do you go when you want a rumor started?

Well, if you're me, you turn to your first post-college crush and first PR teacher and gossip-monger extraordinaire, AMcC.

As will soon become apparent, there was never anything wrong with me when I was locked up for all those months on psych units...

In fact, I made the most of my time in hospitals. When I was at Hall-Brooke in Westport, CT, I told a doctor that I was in the habit of telling plausible lies that I intended to make come true at some point in the future.

So, even if it was racism in the workplace that put a stop to my career at Time Inc., I choose to believe that my bosses were really working in my best interests. They saw my ambition & knew that the culture at Time Inc. would not allow me to succeed on my own terms, so they said to themselves, "He may hate us for a few years ... maybe even a decade or more ... but we're going to force Hicks out of the company, and that way, it will become necessary for him to decide what he really wants to do with his life. He's got bigger things in store for himself than a career selling advertising, anyway."

That's the angle I'm pitching to some big-name journalists -- offering to take them to lunch to discuss a free-lance assignment under their byline to run in the Dartmouth Alumni Magazine. Stay tuned.

13- LETTER TO BLACK ENTERPRISE

February 7, 2009

Mr. Butch Graves

Black Enterprise

130 Fifth Avenue, #10

New York, NY 10011

Dear Butch:

We met at a 1990 Magazine Publishers of America-sponsored event for blacks in publishing at the Howard Inn in Washington, DC.

I've read your father's book and am a subscriber to your publication.

I've also launched a business that, with your help, can assist the current administration in solving the many problems left behind by Bush II.

As you will see in the enclosed documents, I have some legal background, plus experience in real estate, public relations, retailing, magazine publishing, the theater business, insurance and now management & diversity consulting.

My father is a retired Air Force Colonel . He didn't leave me a business to run, but he did pass on to me an appreciation of the need for public service. In my opinion, the President is limited in his ability to effect the changes that need to be made in this country. He can call the tune, but it is up to the business community and private citizens to join the chorus.

I would very much like the chance to sit down and talk with you, perhaps in your office, perhaps at the Yale Club, sometime soon.

Please read the enclosed materials and expect my call.

Best personal regards,

B. C. Hicks

Invisible Man Enterprises

14- FEAR OF A BLACK PLANET

3/9/09

In the eyes of white folks, blacks are fine when they are babies or young children. At that age, they're cute just like chimpanzees at the zoo are cute.

When blacks mature into puberty and beyond, something changes in the dynamic between blacks and whites. Suddenly, blacks are no longer cute and harmless. They now are competition for girls, for coveted spots in AP classes, colleges and, later, jobs and promotions.

After holding a monopoly on status, money & power for so many generations in this country, white people (males, especially) have grown accustomed to lording over blacks and other people of color in much the same way Americans in general regard themselves as separate from, and superior to, the citizens of other nations.

The trouble with this way of thinking is that blacks who came of age after the Civil Rights era were raised by parents who told them that they had to be better than whites in order to earn an equal chance at success. Here's how Chris Rock explained the situation. He said: "If I was as funny as David Spade, I wouldn't eat."

Black intellectuals, athletes, actors & businesspeople who rise to the top of their fields get there by proving themselves against whites jealously defending their spots in the elite – and against naysaying blacks who say either that striving for success is "acting white," or that these blacks' ambitions for themselves are unrealistic and unattainable.

This capitalist society rewards those who are able to "build a better mousetrap." Top producers in America tend to be entrepreneurs -- self-made men and women of all races, creeds and nationalities – with the ability to come up with and sell the best ideas, and the confidence to strike out on their own, rather than work for someone else.

My father, who was born at the tail end of the Depression, doesn't understand my need to work for myself. For him and others of his generation, success meant a "good government job" – one that provides health insurance benefits while you're working and a pension when you retire. He bought into the program whole hog: my father spent 27 years in the U.S. Air Force, retiring in 1986 as a full Colonel; he later got another federal job -- this time in the Justice Department, where he spent another 13 years or so doing administrative work for the Magistrate Judges' division of the U.S. Courts. In retirement, he's not living the life of a successful black entrepreneur such as Earl Graves, Sr., founder of *Black Enterprise* magazine, but given the opportunities available to blacks at the time he was coming of age, I'd say he has done very well for himself.

Blacks of my generation can and should set higher goals. I'm the first person in my family to get an Ivy League education – and I didn't go to Dartmouth College to learn how to be somebody's employee. As I told a former colleague of mine who is still writing for FORTUNE after all these years, "Shame on you for doing the same thing for all this time. FORTUNE writes about business titans and gives you a blueprint for becoming one yourself. If a gold watch is all you want out of your career at FORTUNE, then a gold watch is all you deserve."

For some people, achieving a certain measure of status at a place like FORTUNE and then holding onto that spot in the company for dear life is the best they are capable of, and the perks lavished on senior people at FORTUNE and elsewhere in Time Inc. can sometimes cause the recipients of those perks to forget why they're showing up at the office. For them, the job becomes more about sustaining themselves in their own comfort than creating a world-class quality work-product.

The former colleague of my example is more talented than that: he's a Princeton graduate who got fat & happy, became a creature of habit and stopped reinventing himself.

He's a brand name now, so it's possible for him to get by without doing the hard work of delivering, issue after issue, useful management information to FORTUNE readers. There are no winners in this scenario. The magazine falls short of the tradition of quality it's been known for since its February, 1930 debut issue, so readers and advertisers lose. The writer, who should be fired or reassigned or sent on an extended vacation, continues to take up space on the editorial staff, so younger, hungrier writers who might have turned in better work are forced to wait in line for the chance to do what they do best.

This phenomenon of creature comforts on the job

stifling creativity & innovation, causing a glut of mediocre talent among top managers, and hindering the advancement of younger talent, is a problem not just at Time Inc.; it's present throughout corporate America and it's symptomatic of the white male elite's aversion to competition that has developed over generations. It wasn't such an evident problem when the United States was the world's undisputed economic leader, but in today's increasingly competitive global economy, American companies do themselves and all of their constituents a disservice when they draw upon only the white male segment of the talent pool in their search for a CEO. Look at it this way: if you are a white male and you inherited your money, or you entered an Ivy League school as a legacy, or you ascended to CEO on the good graces of the old-boy network, or all of the above, then you are probably not the killer that your black or female or immigrant peer is.

During my years on the publishing staff at FORTUNE, I was a cocky, successful and very young black male who bore more than a passing resemblance to Mike Tyson. I had been advised by a female colleague on the sales staff that if I wasn't on the verge of being fired every now and then, I wasn't going about my job aggressively enough. While minding my own business and turning in the best work I was capable of at FORTUNE, I was unwittingly creating enemies. In staid, tradition-bound, "birds of a feather flock together" Time Inc., unfamiliarity breeds mistrust and contempt. My colleagues at FORTUNE had an irrational fear of me simply because they had never encountered the likes of me before. Rather than take the opportunity to step outside their comfort zones and get to know me, they let their fear grow into hatred, and then they found a way to get rid of me.

This is one reason why I agree with Attorney General Eric Holder when he says that Americans are cowards when it comes to confronting racial issues.

Another example: some Dartmouth classmates of mine remain mum for weeks after receiving essays I have written that look into the ways people of different races interact with each other. It seems that if I can't be the carefree, beer-drinking, non- intellectual (and, therefore, non-threatening) black person they remember from college, they are unwilling or unable or afraid to engage in conversation with me.

The election of Barack Obama makes me believe that, privately, Americans' hearts are in the right place on questions of race – but, like the young schoolgirl who's never been kissed, they're a little slow on the uptake.

As Bill Cosby said in another context: "Come on, people!!!"

Just invite us into your world: you may find you like us.

15- Email Exchange

--- *Original Message*

From: "B. C. Hicks"

To: "John Clark"

Sent: Wednesday, March 11, 2009 10:15 AM

Subject: Fear of a Black Planet

John,

Here are my current thoughts on Attorney General Eric Holder's remark that Americans are cowards when it comes to addressing the issue of race. Please share it with your friend at the *Wall Street Journal* you told me about and see if he'll advocate for it ...

Thx. BCH

--- *On Mon, 3/16/09, John Clark wrote:*

From: John Clark

Subject: Re: Fear of a Black Planet

To: "B. C. Hicks"

Date: Monday, March 16, 2009, 7:44 PM

B. C.: I have read this piece with interest, although I suggest you must more sharply focus your message. You dismiss more than a generation of affirmative action at the university and corporate level. I do not believe that blacks necessarily have to be better (I don't think David Spade is funny, period), but they do have to be good at what they do, and that is partly a function of education. Your dad came of age as the civil rights movement was getting started (the book I mentioned credits the 1970s with the genuine gains, not the '50s or '60s when the action was going on). The Air Force was a good career choice for him in terms of civil rights because the Air Force was better balanced regarding race than America in general. Colin Powell said the Army was a good job, too. They both showed that they had the goods, and were promoted for that reason.

You put your finger on a greater problem in terms of black progress regarding "acting white."

The Obamas faced the charge of being "elitist" because they speak like educated people. Deriding education and good grades has hurt black progress more than desperate whites trying to keep their positions. This is an excellent area for you to address, as Bill Cosby has--if not in the most positive way.

I have decided that the greatest obstacle to racial progress is ignorance. Not enough people know many people of different races because they don't work together or go to the same schools. I'm not holding my breath for all Americans to have Gale Sayers-Brian Piccolo relationships but knowing each other and respecting each other for the things they do is enough. Holder was wrong, and foolish to use the word "coward." President Obama's election shows that Americans are farther along than we might have thought. Finally, not all people are cut out to be entrepreneurs. Your friend at Fortune, however, could have cut out his own domain. That's entrepreneurial in a way.

I hope these comments are helpful. I'll get to your other essays.

Best,

John

--- *On Tue, 3/17/09, B. C. Hicks wrote:*

From: B. C. Hicks

Subject: Cosby/Jackie Robinson Foundation Awards dinner/Fear of a Black Planet

To: "John Clark"

Date: Tuesday, March 17, 2009, 12:17 PM

John,

Holder was not wrong to use the word "coward." You overlook my point that my Dartmouth friends steer clear of any conversation having to do with the points I raise in my essays. I have grown since college, in part because of my experiences at Vibe and on psychiatric units, where I encountered people from all races and all walks of life. My friends seem to want to deal with the "elitist" B. C. they remember from college ... the one who fits in with the white kids and says nothing to offend them. This is typical of most Americans.

The fact that they elected Barack Obama shows they were smart enough not to fall for McCain's bullshit ... it had nothing to do with race. It had everything to do with a comparison of the candidates' visions for the country. One expressed hope for the future and the need for change; one promised more of the same morally

61

bankrupt, failed policies of Bush II. Like in a relationship with that special someone you love, it takes constant nurturing and work to keep it flourishing. Electing Obama was the first baby step. What remains to be seen is whether or not Americans will continue to venture out of their comfort zones & widen their social and professional circles, or take the "cowardly" route Holder & I agree most are pre-disposed to take.

BCH

16- SWEET LORRAINE

4/22/09

Boyfriend or no boyfriend, Lorraine, that first night we met, you told me you had been an English major in college and that you enjoyed reading and making comments on what you had read … it was then that I gave you some writing samples, along with my email address. I'm pretty sure you've read the stuff (and I <u>know</u> you read the psych essay), but I'm still waiting to hear from you. I know that entering a correspondence with me on subjects I've thought and felt deeply about involves intimacy that you might not feel comfortable with at the moment … but entering that kind of exchange with me does not mean you're cheating on your boyfriend. I have relationships with some of my friends' wives that are in no way physical, but they are deeper in some ways than the relationships they have with their husbands. One college friend told me to stop calling his house and asking to speak to his wife. I said, "She's my friend, too. We were friends in college before you were married. I was at your wedding, remember? I was there as much for her as I was for you."

So ... I'm interested in your reactions to some of the things you've read ... and I'd like to see some stuff that you've been inspired to write. You told me that one of the customers here had some literary connections and had offered to help you.

Well, my connections in the magazine world are pretty good, too. Maybe we can work together to get you published.

Best

BCH

(a message to my favorite bartender at Smith Brothers, Ridgewood, NJ)

17- "We Gave You the White House, for Chrissakes ... What More Do You People Want?"

3/19/09

Don't forget that the United States is "one nation, under God, indivisible ... etc., etc." There is no "we" and "you;" there is only "we."

By electing Barack Obama the first black President of the United States, Americans stepped out of their comfort zone temporarily and, for the first time in the nation's history, entrusted the highest office in the land to someone other than a white male.

But the 2008 election was much more about contrasting messages than it was about race. Obama articulated a vision of hope for America's future and stressed the need to change the way Washington works. McCain promised to continue along the morally bankrupt path to failure blazed by the Bush II administration.

A Brooklyn fireman told me in October, 2008 that he was a staunch Republican and "100% behind McCain."

I replied, "If you're still with McCain at this stage of the game, you're either racist or stupid."

By putting Barack Obama in office, Americans demonstrated that they weren't stupid … but it's far too early for self-congratulation or pronouncements like, "Race is no longer an issue."

Just look at the way we live in this country … do most of us reside in multi-ethnic cities like New York – or in racially homogeneous enclaves like my old hometown of Ridgewood, NJ and my college friends' towns of choice: Weston and Wilton, CT?

The rhetoric of equal opportunity and universal welcome for people of all races is nothing more than an ideal – a goal. In reality, we live in a country where it's OK to go to school with them, to socialize with them and, increasingly, to work with them, but when I go home, I choose to be among my own. Even in places like the Hamptons, where people can afford to live anywhere, many blacks choose to create a neighborhood for themselves in a section of Sag Harbor. The same is true of the Inkwell on Martha's Vineyard.

Growing up in a military family, I had no such choices. My father was a career officer in the U.S. Air Force, so it was typical for me to be the only black kid in an overwhelmingly white neighborhood. When I was 12, my father was still in the Air Force, but we lived off base for the first time in a house our family purchased in Colorado Springs, CO. It was a nice neighborhood – not wealthy, but very comfortable – and similar to military housing in that it was a development comprised of about 4 varieties of model homes, so the houses looked the same, which was familiar. The refreshing change was that I was no longer the only minority. There were Mexicans in the neighborhood.

About four years later, my parents were divorced, and I chose to live with my mother. We rented a modest home in the part of Ridgewood where most of the blacks lived, and, in my junior year of high school, I got my first exposure to wealth. Railroad tracks run through the town of Ridgewood, and the rich kids, for the most part, lived on the West side of the tracks.

There is wealth on the East side, too, but my

neighborhood, on the East side and right on top of the tracks, was the part of town that in status-conscious Ridgewood, nobody wanted to admit they were from.

It was an especially difficult adjustment for me because all of my life I had been the "exceptional black" in elite white neighborhoods. Now, for the first time, I was just another black kid in the black middle-class section of a wealthy white town.

My job, as I saw it, was to scratch and claw my way back into the elite. But in Ridgewood, kids in the elite had money that I didn't have and couldn't get. I knew kids who drove their own brand- new Audis and Alfa Romeos; if I was lucky, I would sometimes get to borrow my mother's reliable old Volvo or my grandmother's big four-door Cadillac.

As the new black kid in town, my approach to life was to "defy the stereotype." I was out to differentiate myself from the blacks that Ridgewood kids had been exposed to – the ones they knew in person, and the images presented to them by the media.

My message was: "I'm not like them ... I have more in common with you."

Now, back to the election of Barack Obama ... and

how this somehow means we live in a color-blind society.

Don't even try it, America.

Not until everyone in this country has walked "a mile in my moccasins" and navigated the social, racial and economic terrain in America that Barack Obama has, that Massachusetts governor Deval Patrick has, that Newark, NJ mayor Cory Booker has, will we live in a so-called "post-racial society," and I'm not sure such a thing is even possible or desirable.

There is a reason conservatives in the United States are so in love with the Constitution and the Declaration of Independence: they are documents that were written of, by and for the landed aristocracy in this country. For all of its egalitarian rhetoric, the Constitution has resulted in an economic and political system that, for close to 250 years, was run exclusively by white males. We speak the language of equal opportunity in America, but the reality has been that rich white males have ruled this country from the beginning and have acted to sustain themselves in the elite for all this nation's history.

How else could someone as mediocre as George W. Bush get accepted at Yale, drink and snort his way through an undistinguished career, sober up, become born again, and then get elected and re-elected to the Presidency?

That's not something to be proud of, conservatives. That's a disgrace. And it reveals a flaw in a Constitution that is ostensibly a "living document," with provisions to be amended to fit the needs of a changing nation, but which has not lived up to its ideals.

"What more do I want?," you ask?

I'd like to live in a nation that passes laws that mean what they say they mean. Abraham Lincoln signed the Emancipation Proclamation in 1863.

Emancipate: To free; to make sovereign.

So why was it such a struggle 100 years later for Martin Luther King, Jr. to get the Civil Rights Act and Voting Rights Act passed? And I've just been talking about the federal government. The real problem and greatest opportunity for change in this country resides in the business community – particularly that segment of the business community with which I am most familiar: the media and entertainment industry.

Big media companies are among the most egregious offenders when it comes to employing staffs that represent the many communities that make up this country. These companies have the power to very quickly educate the nation and the world about the many racial, ethnic and religious populations in America, but if the people in the top jobs all live on Park Avenue, or Westchester County, NY or Fairfield County, CT, the result is programming, movies & editorial content that reflects a very narrow worldview.

If you were a Martian or a foreigner, and you got all your information and entertainment from the big American media companies, you would think Barack and Michelle Obama were the only black Ivy Leaguers who had made something of their lives. Here again, the "exceptional black" syndrome rears its ugly head.

Monday night, I attended my first-ever Jackie Robinson Foundation Awards dinner, a black-tie event at the Waldorf- Astoria emceed by Bill Cosby. Honorees included Robert Redford, Robin Roberts of *Good Morning America* and Dr. Ben Carson, Sr., a black neurosurgeon and professor of neurosurgery from Johns Hopkins University. The stars of the evening, however, were the Jackie Robinson Foundation scholars and alums – young black people from all over the country being given a chance to enter the arena and compete on equal footing with people from this country's elite. Some scholars attend Ivy League schools, but the majority do not. This was a room full of "exceptional blacks" for whom there are no limits. The scholars and alums I met have the brains, the ambition and, thanks to the Jackie Robinson Foundation, the opportunity to change this country and the world – but where was the media coverage?

The star power and the positive energy in the room that night would have made for a great telecast, and if the media in this country were truly liberal as conservatives like to charge, the Jackie Robinson Foundation Awards dinner would be an annually televised event, just like the Oscars, the Emmys and the Tonys. Another thing: if media companies were as liberal as right-wingers charge, I would have had the top job at Time Inc. over a decade ago. Reginald K. Brack, Jr., Time Inc.'s former Chairman, was never in my league as an advertising salesman, writer or manager, but when I made the case that I should replace him, the backlash was swift and strong … and it came from every quarter – even from the people who claim to know and love me best.

Make no mistake, we live in a country that views

"exceptional blacks" as other and dangerous ... and these attitudes are reinforced by a media establishment that includes people like Mr. "I Hope He Fails" Rush Limbaugh.

Why wasn't Rush banned from the airwaves after that one like black radio personality Star of *Star and Buckwild* was banned for calling things as he saw them?

A liberal media would not be in the business of censoring and marginalizing "exceptional blacks." The big image and content producers in this country have a long way to go in the area of diversity and they know it. Rupert Murdoch, Chairman and CEO of News Corp. (owner of FoxNews) won't answer his phone unless the caller knows the name of his assistant. Insular shops like that put out propaganda, not journalism, and NewsCorp is not the only offender. If the three major business publications: FORTUNE, Forbes & BusinessWeek were really doing their jobs -- talking about American competitiveness in the world economy, good corporate governance and social responsibility -- instead of doing puff pieces on celebrity CEOs, there wouldn't have been a market niche for the magazine DiversityInc to enter and exploit. If FORTUNE, Forbes & BusinessWeek had greater diversity of talent and opinions represented in their management and editorial staffs, the content they produce would be more reflective of what's really happening in American business ... and it would be more useful to its readers.

Recently, during a conversation in a Ridgewood, NJ bar, a blue-collar Republican said to me: "You live in Newark ... what are you doing all the way up here?"

I replied: "I'm here to make you uncomfortable." Americans demonstrated the ability to step outside of our comfort zones temporarily when we elected Barack Obama President..

It's an open question as to whether we will stay out of our comfort zones and seek further enlightenment ... or follow the intellectually lazy course of retreating back to our safe enclaves.

Is America inclined, finally, to commit to broadening its horizons, or, as Attorney General Eric Holder observed recently, are we a nation of "cowards" when it comes to addressing the issue of race?

18- BLACK LOVE

4/30/09

It is so gratifying after all these years to be embraced as a peer by the black community. Black social life is not burdened with the trivial games of one-upsmanship you find so often in the Ivy League and in corporate America. Think Public Enemy: "Brothas gonna work it out …"

Brothas been catchin' heck from The Man for so many years in this country that when we spend time together in the barber shops & beauty parlors, drinking & dining establishments, and the churches in the 'hood, we're so busy "tryin' to get over" that it doesn't occur to us to spend our energies putting down our fellow man.

In Carnell's barber shop, located on 16th Avenue in Newark, NJ, just across the street from the buildings my grandmother has owned for years, there is a chess board set up (and always in use), there are current magazines scattered around, there is art on the walls (including artwork made in school by kids in the neighborhood), there is music playing … and there is a bookshelf with not very many, but some of the most interesting titles I've ever seen in one place.

Last time I was in, Carnell told me he had heard once that if you want to hide something from the black man, put it between the covers of a book. He went on to say that he wasn't gonna be one of those niggas to get fooled. "I'm crackin' that motherfucka open," he said. "Ain't nobody puttin' one over on me."

I don't even need a haircut today, but I'm gonna drop by and see what's up. It's the kind of place I find inspiration, and that's why I say that to do your best work, the last place you need to go is a skyscraper in Midtown Manhattan. Been there, done that.

My office is anywhere I happen to be at the moment … with or without my cell phone or computer. These days, with the advent of flash drives, you can carry an enormous number of documents, video clips and songs around with you in your pocket … stop into a FedEx/Kinko's or UPS store … or any internet café … plug in and fire out emails – with or without attachments, print a few things, if necessary … and make copies that you can personalize with handwritten notes, stick 'em in an envelope, drop them off at the home or office of whoever it is you are trying to reach, and keep on steppin'.

Fuck whoever wrote the "7 Habits of Highly Effective People." As I say in another piece I wrote: "a creature of habit, by definition, is not an innovator."

Fuck FORTUNE too, by the way. Yesterday, I was in the Time & Life Building, a place I've been banned from since 1998 – but I'm the Invisible Man, remember – so I've learned to slip in and out whenever I want. Anyway, in the reception area, I came across a brand-new issue of FORTUNE with Warren Buffett on the cover, singing the praises of the Electric Vehicle. It seems the Oracle of Omaha has looked into the future and seen bright prospects for this technology – so all you investors, "Get on board."

Maybe if the backward-assed, Midwestern motherfuckin' rube had looked into the past – specifically, to the March 8, 1993 issue of FORTUNE – he would have lent his credibility to this green industry sooner, and people like Mr. "Fossil-Fuel- Proponent-in-an-Alternative-Fuels-Economy" Alex Taylor III (FORTUNE's dinosaur of an Automotive Editor) and his friends in Detroit wouldn't have launched their conspiracy to nip an emerging market in the bud, resulting in the situation chronicled in the documentary film, "Who Killed the Electric Vehicle?"

When I was at FORTUNE, in the era of James B. Hayes and Marshall Loeb, the magazine's slogan was "Inside the Mind of Management" and FORTUNE ran cover stories like: "The King is Dead," "Bureaucracy Busters" and "How America Can Triumph."

Today, FORTUNE is so useless and out of touch, I really don't know where to begin. That was another reason I visited the Time & Life Building. I wasn't there for my health ... I was there as a journalist and businessman trying to offer my expertise. Hear that, Ann Moore, you fucking ignoramus? You are not in my league, you know it, so not only do you not answer my phone calls or engage me in a conversation to find out what it is I want to talk to you about ... you send Time Inc. Security to escort me out of the building. But when I tell them, "Ok, I'm leaving. My work here today is done," they tell me to sit down, which I refuse to do (I've got places to go, things to do elsewhere) and then proceed to physically and violently wrestle me to the ground, Keystone Kops style, put handcuffs on me, perp-walk me through the lobby of the Time & Life Building and take me for a short elevator ride and detain me in a holding cell.

Really, Ann? Is that the way Henry Luce's once-proud "journalistic enterprise" conducts its business these days under your stewardship? You're so afraid of the truth and so afraid of "exceptional blacks" that you adopt an overseer mentality and break out the whips and chains?

You backward-assed, superior, affirmative action hire … don't you realize it's a new day in America?

What if Barack Obama or Eric Holder came to visit?

I bet they'd get the royal treatment … but in the back of your mind, I'm sure you'd be thinking: "How can Dick Parsons and I use our properties to advance the interests of the Republican Party and get ourselves a nice, wholesome, family- values espousing (read: "white") woman like Sarah Palin or a former preacher-man like FoxNews' Mike Huckabee into the White House and thereby bring back the 'good-ole-boy' days in America?"

You and your ilk are so averse to calling a black man 'sir,' you can't see straight. Bet you felt the same way about Colin Powell, you smug, superior, once-closeted, now exposed racists.

Ok, Ann Moore of the 34th floor, stay rooted in the past and don't listen to what I have to say. Get your advice from Time Inc. Editor-in-Chief John Huey, another head-in-the-sand-having chump who won't respond to my letters or phone calls, and see where that gets you.

For the rest of America and the American-media-consuming world who want to learn something, I recommend that you steer clear of Time Inc. publications. You want useful business information for today's climate? Skip FORTUNE. Read FASTCOMPANY.

19- LETTER TO TIME

March 11, 2009

Mr. Mark Halperin

TIME

Time & Life Bldg

Rockefeller Center

New York, NY 10020

Dear Mark:

I submit that mine is a voice that needs to be aired nationally on issues of race in society and in the workplace.

Part of what I'd like to do in my practice as a diversity consultant is speak to audiences like the one you addressed as a moderator on Monday night.

My target is the information & entertainment industry, because they are the most egregious offenders in the area of diversity & because, as shapers of opinion, they are in a position to do the most good.

Having D.L. Hughley as part of that speakers' group is a good start ... but don't stop there. He's a comic ... I represent a black business constituency and the Ivy League.

Even if you can't use this piece this time, please keep me in mind as a resource when issues of race come up in your reporting – and please submit this piece on my behalf to the people you work with on the speakers' series & tell them I'm throwing my hat in the ring to be another black voice …

As a bonus, I am including information on the collection of essays that I'm trying to publish as a Time Inc. employment memoir. I am a casualty of the company's failure to follow through on its good intentions (best case scenario), or of its exclusionary old-boy network that values white mediocrity over black excellence (worst case scenario).

Please get back to me with comments. Thanks very much.

Best,

B. C. Hicks

Invisible Man Enterprises

20- HEALTH CARE

2/18/09

Hillary Clinton's presidential bid fell short, but her health care study group from the early 1990s has borne fruit.

My long fight against a misdiagnosis of bipolar disorder has resulted in a report that can form the beginning of a comprehensive health care policy initiative for the nation.

I've been out of college 21 years, and 13-1/2 of those years have been spent studying health care as it is delivered in psychiatric hospitals in 3 states (Connecticut, New York & New Jersey), and outpatient psychiatric care in a fourth state (Virginia). I've logged close to 18 months as a patient on locked psychiatric units over this period -- in private, state & city hospitals.

During this time, I earned licenses to sell health insurance in New York & New Jersey – and I believe private insurers can help solve the budget shortfalls that plague so many of our health care providers. Private insurers have billions in "reserves" which says to me that they are holding in reserve monies that could be used to offset the financial burdens under which too many health care consumers labor. It also says to me that they have been overcharging policyholders for decades on end. As the adage goes, "Behind every fortune there lies a great crime."

Health care insurers make money hand over fist selling "Medi- Gap" policies that supplement the coverage of those who have Medicare, but they contribute little or nothing to the job of keeping Medicare solvent. Also, "Charity Care" is something the private sector can and should contribute to, rather than letting the burden fall on city and state governments.

FORTUNE magazine ran a feature called "Your Money at Play" in an issue which had on its cover a story chronicling "The New Jobless." To me, this is a demonstration of how callous the rich and the employed are when it comes to those in need. There was a "we're gonna pull through this together" ethic in this country during the time of the Depression that needs to come back in this age of the Internet. Candidate Obama tapped into that spirit of community when he raised those massive sums in online campaign contributions, but as

President, his rhetoric has changed, and Washington is behaving as it always has.

The legacy of Bush-Cheney is that companies and individuals who want to participate in this most open of economies will now be forced to pay a price that they haven't previously been asked to pay. I don't agree that the federal government should, as a first resort, be handing out these "rescue packages." Hedge funds, investment banks, insurance companies, universities, insurance profiteer Warren Buffett & the many new billionaires this country has produced over the past decade or so need to be pressed into service.

Warren Buffett's company, Berkshire Hathaway, owns the Kirby brand of vacuum cleaners. Kirbys are American made in a factory in Ohio and sold door-to-door by independent distributors. For about two weeks last summer, I worked for a Kirby distributor in North Arlington, NJ and was very impressed with the commitment the Kirby sales force brought to the job of representing the product and the company. I met some good salespeople when I worked for Time Inc., but not one of them can hold a candle to the best Kirby distributors.

These people work six days a week, they carry heavy equipment door to door and demonstrate the product in prospective customers' homes. If the Kirby doesn't sell after a demonstration, the distributor must quickly clean and pack the Kirby back into the box so that it is pristine and ready for the next demonstration. The best Kirby distributors make a good living and so are able to self-fund their health coverage, but given all of the insurance companies Warren Buffett owns or controls and given all of the sweat equity Kirby distributors bring to their job – every day, six days a week – I think it is a crime that Warren Buffett does not provide health coverage for his Kirby distributors. (Another example of how far removed the high and mighty are from the real-life concerns of their employees and ordinary citizens.)

21- LETTER TO STEERFORTH PRESS

April 27, 2009

Mr. Chip Fleischer

Publisher

Steerforth Press

Lebanon, NH

Dear Chip:

I named my company **Invisible Man Enterprises** because I was inspired by the Ralph Ellison novel.

It tells the story of a Harlem streetcorner orator like Malcolm X, who spoke to rapt audiences and successfully led a movement ... but the beauty of the novel is that it tells the story without ever relating what it was that the Invisible Man said.

That's where I come in.

The book I would like you to consider publishing is entitled <u>Notes From the Asylum: What Ralph Ellison's "Invisible Man" Actually Said</u>.

The Grateful Dead had a tune, "What A Long, Strange Trip It's Been," to which I say a hearty "Amen."

As you will learn from reading the essay, **"Comedy,"** which will be included in the book, to this day, it remains a mystery to me who was responsible for ending my career at Time Incorporated. All I know is that nobody in that company can tell me I left because I was a failure or that I was incapable of performing the duties I was required to fulfill as an Advertising Sales Representative at FORTUNE or as the founding Classified Manager at Vibe. Ever since my last day at Vibe, in the fall of 1994 (I remained on the payroll until March, 1995), I have been reflecting on and writing about my experiences at Time Inc., which is the company I wanted to work for since college. These musings resulted in the collection of essays that started us talking, and, since that writing is too good to have gone unpublished for such a long time, my suspicion is that the publishing rights were actually purchased by someone who never intended to release the book.

The process of launching my company, Invisible Man Enterprises, and trying to get my Time Inc employment memoir published so that I would have a "deliverable" to leave behind with potential consulting clients, resulted in the thinking and writing that comprise **Notes From the Asylum**.

Much of the writing was done while I was a patient on locked psychiatric units, matching wits with psychiatrists who were convinced that the stories I related to them about my Time Inc. career were untrue and proof that I was "grandiose," "delusional," suffering from bi-polar disorder and in need of hospitalization & medication.

So far, only their side of the story has been told ... and I believe that's unfair.

It's impossible to win an argument if I am unable to get my words in print – and that's where I am hoping you will come in.

I look forward to the chance to discuss this project with you in greater detail after you've read what I have sent.

Thanks very much.

Best,

B. C. Hicks

Invisible Man Enterprises

22- COMEDY

4/27/09

From a literary critic's point of view, "comedy" is the action that ensues when an obstacle – physical (like a wall), or imaginary (like an edict, such as "under penalty of death, or 5 years in prison, you must not cross this line") – is erected between a female and male protagonist, one or both of whom are determined to breach that obstacle to see where a conversation or a relationship might lead.

In the case of me and Sarah L., a nurse I met while a patient at Hall-Brooke psychiatric hospital in Westport, CT, the obstacle and the legal jeopardy associated with crossing that line directly, in the manner a lovelorn brute might go about things, are very real indeed.

But what I have going for me are my very vivid memories of the brief snippets of conversations we had when I was there, the interactions I know that she witnessed between myself and my friends who came to visit me (sometimes bearing gifts, such as khaki slacks, shorts and a denim shirt by Polo – Ralph Lauren & a beautiful sport shirt and polo shirt by Vineyard Vines), the notes and letters I sent to her attention at Hall-Brooke following my release & the actual visits I made to Hall-Brooke, with the intention of seeing her, giving her small tokens of my affection that I had purchased with her in mind, and seeing where those brief snippets of conversations I mentioned earlier might lead over drinks at a place like Mario's or Tarantino's, near the Westport train station.

As I have said in a message to a close friend from college, someone feels threatened by the prospect of Sarah and me communicating and perhaps embarking on a friendship or romance growing out of what began as a patient-nurse relationship.

Some lawyer relative of Sarah's called a college friend of mine, Bob Mitchell, '87, whose family owns and operates the clothing store Mitchells of Westport, and threatened dire consequences for me should I continue in my pursuit of Sarah. (I believe the man placed this call to the Mitchell home, spooking both Bobby and his wife, Karen).

Bob and Karen dismissed all of the direct interactions

they've had in their relationship with me over the years because they felt their "cute Connecticut lifestyle" threatened by this two-bit lawyer who knows only three things about me: 1) I'm black, 2) I'm a former psychiatric patient at Hall-Brooke and 3) I'm interested in pursuing a relationship with his relative, Sarah L.

What the man doesn't know about me could fill a book – maybe two. Even though I never went to law school, I did spend time as an intern in the New York, Washington, DC & Boston offices of the law firm Skadden, Arps, Slate, Meagher & Flom while I was an undergraduate at Dartmouth College.

Further, I've been a chess player since about the age of 8, I am a fan & student of the theater, and I am a media and entertainment executive of the highest order. From the Broadway cast recording of "Purlie," starring Cleavon Little, which is in my car, I know that "There's More Than One Way of Skinnin' a Cat."

This guy has no clue what he is up against, so my approach is to give him the benefit of the doubt and think to myself, "forgive this poor soul, for he knows not with whom he is fucking."

If he took the time to get to know me, rather than

lash out and disturb my nervous-Nellie friends, he'd probably learn that we have some things in common & perhaps find out some things about me that he likes or even admires.

This chump is not even on my radar screen.

The adversaries I am interested in identifying and vanquishing are my former colleagues at Time Inc. who knew me, knew something about my capabilities and decided to cross me anyway.

The manner in which they chose to attack was devious and surreptitious, so, to this day, I don't know everyone who was involved. All I know is that I was injured by my association with Time Incorporated for no other reasons than I was black, good at my job and more comfortable around white people than my colleagues were around me.

As I have said privately and in a letter to a filmmaker I respect, Time Inc. "took a leap of faith when it put a woman, Ann Moore, in the top job, but to this day, the culture in that company would resist elevating me, or anybody black, to the job of CEO, regardless of qualifications. Richard Parsons, Chairman of Time Warner, is another problem: 1) he came from banking and the Time Warner board, so he's not even a media executive; 2) once Parsons was promoted from the board to a top management position at Time Warner, he followed Clarence Thomas' example of slamming shut the doors of opportunity that he went through."

When I was released from Vibe magazine after refusing a promotion that would have required me to sell or sublet my West Village apartment and relocate to Detroit, I was told that I had to leave the company – originally without a severance package.

I was able to continue on the payroll at full pay and full benefits for 5 months, but, in order to get the package, I had to forfeit my right to sue the company for discrimination.

I'm only an occasional church-goer, so it is not a belief in God that guides me. Rather, I believe that the universe cares not a whit about the affairs of mankind ... but forces of good and evil are constantly at work in the universe and arrayed against each other in an eternal struggle. It's up to each individual, in every moral dilemma that faces him or her, to choose which army he wants to join.

The fact that mankind has not yet been annihilated in a nuclear holocaust leads me to believe that the forces of good are prevailing.

However, there are people in this world occupying powerful positions in government (to include the intelligence services), the media & the military, whose conception of right and wrong is murky ... and it prevents them from being able to choose a side and stick to it. Sometimes they are fighting on the side of good, but at other times, the interests of the nation require these powerful people to do business with "unsavory characters", spend time "in the shadows" and temporarily join the "evil" army – because they are convinced that this is the only way to advance the national interest, which, of course, is ultimately "good."

This is the "ends justify the means" rationale advocated by former Vice President Dick Cheney, former Secretary of Defense Donald Rumsfeld and others ... but only time will tell whether or not that argument holds water.

The question needs to be asked: what jeopardy attaches should this line of reasoning fail?

Does it even matter in the end?

Are these people and their lawyers so powerful that, once they've attained an office like Vice President or

Secretary of Defense, they are essentially above the law and there is no penalty for any of the "evil" acts they may have committed in the name of the United States of America?

Let's not forget the "Patriot Act," waterboarding, extraordinary renditions & other tools these former officials and their staffs advocated for and employed in their service to the country.

Sometimes, medals are awarded to those who go "above and beyond the call of duty" on behalf of a military or diplomatic objective.

At other times, when tactics are deemed by a military tribunal or the U.S. Supreme Court to be "beyond the pale," prison terms and even executions ensue.

My memory is not so good on this point, but I seem to recall Dick Cheney making the argument that the prison at Guantanamo Bay needed to remain in operation because it is an essential component in the "War on Terror."

Which brings us again to the question of "jeopardy."

I'm wondering whether or not Dick Cheney would go on record and say that he is prepared to enter Guantanamo Bay as an inmate should it be decided that some of the time he and others spent "in the shadows" was spent fighting exclusively on the side of evil and served no meaningful national purpose ... Time will tell. I'm a long-distance runner ... and I'm willing to wait this one out, as I once told my father, a retired Colonel in the U.S. Air Force who later served as an administrator in the Magistrate Judges division of the U.S. Courts. His office was in the Thurgood Marshall Building in Washington, DC.

23- CHER-CHEZ LA FEMME

Sarah (the nurse with the purple scrub pants),

4/22/09

If I had to choose between the Navy and the Marines, I would say "Go Navy," but for the purposes of this note, the Marines have a better motto. It is "Semper Fidelis" (Always faithful). This is my message to you.

BCH

24- Note to Sander Connolly, '87

Sander (Connolly, '87, a neurosurgeon and professor at Columbia-Presbyterian),

4/22/09

You know the rules better than I ... but I suspect it is the hospital, not the nurse, who is behind this complaint that is making it impossible for me to communicate with her. There is a pathological fear in this country concerning black male sexuality. Two examples I've experienced apart from the Hall-Brooke situation illustrate my point ... the first is kind of pathetic, but also very funny in a way: I was sitting at a bar in my old hometown of Ridgewood, NJ and overheard this traumatized white woman telling her friends, "I had a dream last night that Barack Obama raped me." The second involves the young woman who bought my apartment on Perry Street. It was going to be hard for me to leave that place under any circumstances, but when I saw the condition of the apartment after we renovated it, I wanted very badly to figure out a way to keep it instead of selling. Anyway, a few months after I sold, I was at a restaurant in the neighborhood and decided to stop by the building and buzz the old apartment, invite the girl out for a drink and ask her to invite me in so I could see what she had done with the place. This set off alarm bells, and the next thing I know, her father is talking to my father and to the police because she's afraid I intend to rape her. Everyone says I've got to stay away from Perry Street and the West Village. Fucking ridiculous. Anyway, I was hoping you could devise a way to get the second attachment to this message to the Hall-Brooke nurse in question, Sarah L. We had a very rare and intimate and innocent connection during my stay there as a patient, and I always intended to explore how we might get along on the outside after I was released. Someone feels threatened by this ... and I'm confident it is not Sarah. Get back to me. I'd like for us to meet for a beer to catch up on this & other goings-on in our lives.

Best,

BCH

25- Letter to DiversityInc.

November 9, 2011

Mr. Luke Visconti

Partner & Co-Founder

DiversityInc.

570 Broad Street - 15th floor

Newark, NJ 07102

Dear Luke,

I think your magazine is harming, rather than helping the cause of diversity in the American workplace. If workforce diversity is a priority for a corporation, a municipality, a state, or a nation, it should be a priority for that entity's top manager.

The cause of diversity should not be delegated or relegated to a Human Resources department or a 'Diversity' officer ... all that does is add another layer of bureaucracy and give the CEO a scapegoat to hide behind should his company be criticized for its failure to attract, recognize, reward & retain quality people of color.

As a black graduate of an Ivy League college and a businessperson with a lifetime of experiences in addition to being the victim of a failed or abandoned diversity initiative at Time Inc., I bring insights and a perspective to this problem that your magazine's "Ask the White Dude" column cannot.

Finally, since you are neither a psychologist nor a psychiatrist and you haven't been in the same room with me since we were colleagues at FORTUNE, you are in no position to characterize my attempts to contact DiversityInc. as abnormal behavior. I am a diversity consultant, Luke, calling to offer my insights.

Thanks for sending your best wishes for a good future. Frankly, I'd prefer a paid writing assignment. Please read through the attachments and either get back to me or expect a call from me soon.

Best,

B. C. Hicks

Invisible Man Enterprises

26- NOTE TO JEFF BEWKES

Jeff (Bewkes, CEO, Time Warner),

10/28/11

When I was at FORTUNE, my colleague John Needham & I met with Mayo Stuntz, a friend of Steve Ross' who came over from Warner Communications to head up Time Warner Enterprises, a department created to capitalize on "synergies" within the merged companies. John Needham later became head of the newly-created FORTUNE Enterprises before leaving to form his own conferencing business, Needham Partners LLC. Since 1994, when I was asked to leave the company after refusing a promotion at Vibe that would have required me to sell my West Village apartment & relocate to Detroit ... I have been either working in the entertainment industry or writing about race relations in America from the unique perspective of a black person who had a successful (albeit short) career at the highest levels of one of the biggest media & entertainment companies in the world. James B. Hayes, the former publisher of

FORTUNE, hired me into a position that was created to introduce a young black man or woman to the business of magazine publishing. My start date was January 16, 1990, the first day Time Warner began operations following the merger. As I told former Chairman Richard Parsons in a letter dated February 6, 2009, "It could be argued that I never left Time Warner because the entire manuscript of my book was left with [Time Inc.'s book- publishing entity] Little, Brown and with Vibe when that publication was still a unit of Time Inc. Ventures." There has been a lot of money made from projects sourced directly or indirectly from my material, and through it all, I have remained loyal to Time Inc. and Time Warner. I am a Lifetime member of the Time-Life Alumni Society, and I am a Time Warner shareholder. The way I look at things, my company, Invisible Man Enterprises, is Time Warner Enterprises by another name. What I would like to arrive at with you is a fair estimation of the dollar amount I should be compensated for the value I created for this company over the past 16-1/2 years. In addition, I don't think you can find anyone anywhere who is more qualified than I am to help Time Warner address its diversity issues from a position on the Time Warner board. Please read through the materials I've enclosed and expect a call from me soon.

Best,

B. C. Hicks

Invisible Man Enterprises

27- Open letter to Wynton Marsalis:

4/25/09

I own a trumpet and a flugelhorn, Wynton, and pretty soon, I'm gonna buy an electric guitar.

None of this means that I will ever feel comfortable enough in my abilities as a musician to perform onstage.

So what makes you think you can play the role of businessman, raise funds for Jazz at Lincoln Center & choose as your location for the facility One Time Warner Center?

Thought I wouldn't notice, hornplayer?

From now on, I make the rules and you as a musician will have to negotiate with me for what you get paid on gigs.

"FROM THE PLANTATION TO THE PENITENTIARY," you say?

There's an idea, businessman.

Your gig from now until I decide differently is to teach music to inmates in the nation's prisons.

Think **"Jazz for Young People,"** only you'll have older

students, too … and, just like your students, you'll be behind bars.

I've seen some pretty good prison artwork.

Maybe if you demonstrate real commitment to this project, you'll be able to show me some tattoos after a couple of months.

Take that blowhard Stanley Crouch with you … maybe Mr. *"Notes of a Hanging Judge"* will learn something from having the gavel snatched from his hand.

B. C. Hicks, uncredited producer, **The Soloist** … the new Jamie Foxx, Robert Downey, Jr. pic

28- MILITARY-INDUSTRIAL COMPLEX

Was it President Dwight D. Eisenhower who said, "Beware the military-industrial complex"?

Check it.

My father served in the U.S. Air Force and the Justice Department.

My mother was a stockbroker for Merrill, Lynch.

I graduated from both Dartmouth College and the United States Naval Academy, then worked at FORTUNE magazine & New York Life, among other places.

I am the motherfucking military-industrial complex. As Ice-T once said, "You shoulda killed me last year."

29- BUGS & DAFFY

Here's a thought:

I am Bugs because I always win ... But I can relate to Daffy.

I "feel his pain," as former President Bill Clinton used to say.

30- Dangerfield's

Remark made to a horrified audience at Dangerfield's after about 15 minutes of non-stop Triumph, the Insult-Comic Dog-style humor:

"I'm not even a comedian … I'm a mental patient."

my client & one of the "Raging Jews of Comedy," Steve Marshall

About the Author

B. C. Hicks is a graduate of Dartmouth College, an honorary graduate of the United States Naval Academy at Annapolis and a tireless warrior in the civil rights movement that was derailed in the 1960s with the assassinations, most notably of Medgar Evers, Malcolm X, Martin Luther King, Jr. & Robert F. Kennedy. He lives in Manhattan, but also spends time in the surrounding New York, New Jersey & Connecticut cities and suburbs, where he finds inspiration for his journalistic and creative writing endeavors.

Mad Love to My Publicist, Deb Kieke, of Burson-Marsteller in New York.

"It's a Marvelous Night for a Moondance."